ID0906420

The South American Family Table

BY KATHRYN HULICK

CONNECTING CULTURES THROUGH FAMILY AND FOOD

The South American Family Table

By Kathryn Hulick

MASON CREST

Mason Crest
450 Parkway Drive, Suite D
Broomall, PA 19008
www.masoncrest.com

First printing
9 8 7 6 5 4 3 2 1

Series ISBN: 978-1-4222-4041-0
Hardback ISBN: 978-1-4222-4051-9
EBook ISBN: 978-1-4222-7749-2

Produced by Shoreline Publishing Group LLC
Santa Barbara, California
Editorial Director: James Buckley Jr.
Designer: Tom Carling
Production: Patty Kelley
www.shorelinepublishing.com
Front cover: MBI/Shutterstock (top); Sergii Koval/Dreamstime.com (bottom).

Library of Congress Cataloging-in-Publication Data
Names: Hulick, Kathryn, author. Title: The South American family table / by Kathryn Hulick. Description: Broomall,
   PA : Mason Crest, [2018] | Series: Connecting cultures through family and food | Includes index.
Identifiers: LCCN 2018001250| ISBN 9781422240519 (hardback) | ISBN 9781422240410 (series) | ISBN
   9781422277492 (ebook)
Subjects: LCSH: Food habits--South America--Juvenile literature. | Hispanic Americans--Diet--Juvenile literature. |
   Latin America--Social life and customs--Juvenile literature. | United States--Emigration and immigration--Juvenile
   literature.
Classification: LCC GT2853.S63 H85 2018 | DDC 394.1/2098--dc23 LC record available at https://lccn.loc.
   gov/2018001250

QR Codes disclaimer:

Contents

KEY ICONS TO LOOK FOR

 Words to Understand: These words with their easy-to-understand definitions will increase the reader's understanding of the text, while building vocabulary skills.

 Sidebars: This boxed material within the main text allows readers to build knowledge, gain insights, explore possibilities, and broaden their perspectives by weaving together additional information to provide realistic and holistic perspectives.

 Educational Videos: Readers can view videos by scanning our QR codes, providing them with additional educational content to supplement the text. Examples include news coverage, moments in history, speeches, iconic moments, and much more!

 Text-Dependent Questions: These questions send the reader back to the text for more careful attention to the evidence presented here.

 Research Projects: Readers are pointed toward areas of further inquiry connected to each chapter. Suggestions are provided for projects that encourage deeper research and analysis.

 Series Glossary of Key Terms: This back-of-the-book glossary contains terminology used throughout this series. Words found here increase the reader's ability to read and comprehend higher-level books and articles in this field.

Introduction

In South America, penguins flock on the far southern coast, which is not far from Antarctica. Piranhas swim in the wide waters of the Amazon, the largest river in the world. Llamas graze on the slopes of the lofty Andes Mountains. Countless birds, frogs, snakes, and other creatures populate the dense rain forests. As for the South American people, they are as diverse and vibrant as their geography. On this continent, many cultures have mixed.

In the 15th century, native civilizations flourished across the Americas. Then, in 1492, Christopher Columbus arrived. Starting in the Caribbean, Mexico, and Central America, the Spanish began taking over the land from local populations. The Aztecs, Incas, and many other native peoples fell to European diseases and armies. Spain gradually took control of the entire western coast of the newly named continent of South America. Meanwhile, Portugal conquered the land in the northeast, including most of what is now Brazil. The Spanish and Portuguese languages, Catholic religion, and Southern European cooking techniques spread throughout the area, which became known as Latin America.

The Europeans forced many native people to work as slaves. They also brought in slaves from Africa. These populations already had their own cultures, languages, religions, and foods. Though many native traditions were suppressed, some managed to survive, especially in rural areas. And some native foods spread

throughout the world. Corn, potatoes, tomatoes, chocolate, and vanilla all originated in South America.

In the 1800s, South American countries began fighting for their independence. As each new country separated itself from Europe, it gained its own national identity, which mixed European and African cultural traditions and foods with those of the original inhabitants. Meanwhile, immigrants continued to arrive in South America, mainly from Europe, but also from China, Japan, and other parts of Asia. During the 19th and early 20th century, both North and South America became "melting pots" where people from many different backgrounds came together.

South American nations such as Brazil mix European and African traditions.

The flow of people began to reverse in the mid-20th century. Wars, crime, poverty, political upheaval, and economic crises prompted many South Americans to leave. Wherever they went, these immigrants brought with them their rich and diverse culture, including holidays, social customs, and of course, food.

Beef is a big part of most South American countries' cuisine. Here, an Argentine cowboy, called a gaucho, *guides a herd to market.*

Getting Here

Victor Alarcón arrived at his mother-in-law's house one day to find money heaped on the bed. This wasn't a good thing. It was the 1980s in Bolivia, and an economic depression had caused extreme **inflation**, in which money loses value rapidly. The money looked like a lot, but it wasn't worth much. And it would be worth even less in a week. Alarcón's sister-in-law had already moved abroad to

Words to Understand

dictator a leader with total power

economy a region's wealth or resources

emigrant a person who leaves his or her home country to live elsewhere

immigrant a person who has permanently settled in a new country

inflation a trend in which prices increase over time

oppression a long period of harsh treatment

refugee a person forced to leave his or her home country due to war or natural disaster

visa a document that gives a travevler permission to enter and stay in a country

La Paz, Bolivia, is one of the world's highest-altitude capital cities. Located on several levels, parts of the city can be reached via cable cars like these.

the Washington, DC, area. He decided to join her there. He had two young sons and hoped for a better future for his family.

Alarcón's first experience in the Unitd States didn't go well. He walked three miles each way to a grueling job washing dishes at a Mexican restaurant. He depended on his sister-in-law and her husband for everything. Soon, he returned to Bolivia. But two years later, he decided to give America another try. "I was not happy [in Bolivia]," he said later. "Always, in the back of my mind, I was thinking, 'I can do better than this.'" This time, he was better prepared for the reality of life in a new country. He returned to the same restaurant and soon got promoted. A few months later, his wife and children joined him.

A road border crossing from Mexico into the United States is the final passageway for many people arriving from Central America.

Troubled Times

Bolivia wasn't the only nation in South America going through troubled times. Immigrants from Europe had once flocked to South America. But this trend began to reverse during the second half of the 20th century, as one country after another in the region went through political and economic crises. Military **dictators** seized power in several nations. And the economic collapse that Alarcón experienced also spread through other countries. Most people who chose to leave resettled in a nearby South

Guyana and Its Neighbors

A traveler visiting almost any part of South America will hear most people speaking Spanish or Portuguese, and will see mostly Catholic churches. But in a corner of the continent bordering the Caribbean Sea are three tropical countries with very diverse languages and cultures. Guyana, Suriname, and French Guiana were once colonies of Britain, the Netherlands, and France. These

European nations brought in slaves from Africa and India to work on plantations. They also enslaved native South American people. All these groups intermixed. Richard David immigrated to America from Guyana when he was ten years old. He has a Christian father, a Muslim mother, and Hindu grandparents. "That's not uncommon in Guyana," he said. The foods and culture of Guyana are most similar to Caribbean islands that also once had European plantations worked by slaves. Salt fish and bake, a dish of salted cod and fried bread, is one very popular food in this region.

American country with a more stable **economy** or political situation. But others ventured out to more distant destinations in the United States, Canada, Europe, and even Asia.

In Brazil, a military dictatorship ruled the country from 1964 through 1985. During the 1980s, Brazil's economy suffered from **inflation** and unemployment rose steeply. Brazilians began leaving the continent to seek opportunities elsewhere, mainly in the United States , but also in Europe and Japan. Brazil had become the primary destination for Japanese **emigrants** in the 1920s. But by the 1980s and 1990s, Japan was prospering

With Brazil's sizeable Japanese population, event such as this drumming festival in São Paulo are not uncommon.

while Brazil struggled. As a result, many Brazilians of Japanese descent decided to resettle in Japan. Patricia Rodrigues Shibata arrived in 1991. "Japan left me a long way from family and friends," she said. "I was very lonely." But the Brazilian population in Japan was growing rapidly. By 2008, Brazilian barbecue restaurants, called *churrascarias,* had started popping up in Japan. A city to the north of Tokyo became known as "Brazilian town."

A similar relationship has developed between Chile and Sweden. In 1973, Chilean revolutionaries overthrew president Salvador Allende, who had been elected as the region's first socialist leader. His successor, General Augusto Pinochet, became a brutal dictator. Immediately after the takeover, thousands of people who had supported Allende decided it was safest to leave the country. Many went to Sweden, a country that had also supported Allende. Cristian Delgado, who helps run the Swedish-Chilean association, says, "They came due to their political convictions and what

History of Latina American immigration

was happening in the country. . . . They probably thought they'd return to Chile, but many made families here, had kids, married Swedes." Chileans also fled to the United States and Canada. Peru went through a turbulent period beginning in the 1980s, when two separate radical groups began terrorizing the country. For the next two decades, many people left the country. Peruvians now make up the second largest South American population in the United States, after Colombians.

Paraguay and Uruguay

Paraguay and Uruguay are two small South American countries that both border Argentina and Brazil. Though they have similar names and locations, the countries have had different histories. In 1864, Brazil, Argentina, and Uruguay all invaded Paraguay, leading to devastation there. Since then, Paraguay has struggled to develop. Its population is mostly rural and poor, and when they choose to seek opportunities

elsewhere, they tend to move to Argentina. Uruguay, in contrast, managed to attract many European settlers during the end of the 19th century, and was one of the wealthiest countries in South America at the time. But after a military dictatorship that lasted from 1973 to 1985, the economy suffered. Many young, educated people started leaving for better jobs elsewhere. After Fabiana Robuschi finished medical school, she planned to move to Europe. There, she knew she could earn 40 times as much as in Uruguay. "I can't live in my country, where I grew up, where I know the streets, where my family lives," she said.

The Crises Continue

Ecuadorians have been migrating to escape poverty since the 1960s, but an economic crisis in 1999 led to even greater movement. During the 1990s and 2000s, most Ecuadorian emigrants went to Spain. At the time, they didn't need **visas** to enter the country. Sandra Delgado arrived in Spain during this period, and stayed on illegally. She and her husband had left their four children behind. "I would never leave my children a second time," she says. The family was eventually reunited.

The Ecuadorian flag flutters over a colorful scene in the city of Guayaquil.

Argentina went through a military dictatorship that lasted from 1976 through 1983. During this time, many people fled political **oppression**. But for most of Argentina's history, the country has attracted **immigrants** from Europe and other South American countries. It wasn't until an economic crisis in the 2000s that Argentines began leaving in greater numbers for job opportunities elsewhere, mainly in the United States, Italy, Spain, and Israel. Argentina has one of the largest Jewish populations in the world, and these people all have the right to become Israeli citizens. Elias Simana, owner of an advertising agency in Buenos Aires, Argentina, took advantage of this policy in 2002. "Over the previous nine months,

Argentina has a large community of Jewish people, most of whom are descendants of refugees from Europe during and after World War II.

the situation in Argentina had been increasingly problematic for me.... Our final month there was downright dramatic: I knocked on my clients' doors for payment, and my creditors did the same to me. But the payment chain had been shattered. We just couldn't go on anymore." Israel has been very welcoming to Argentine immigrants. The country even offers financial aid to help newcomers get a new start.

Venezuela had been one of the most prosperous nations in South America from the 1920s through the 1970s, thanks to an oil boom. But this nation's economy suffered from inflation along with Bolivia and Brazil during the 1980s and 1990s, prompting many working class people to leave. Then socialist leader Hugo Chavez was elected in 1998, causing some wealthy elites who feared the new government to depart. Recently, Venezuela has entered a new period of crisis. Inflation has skyrocketed and foreign companies have stopped selling goods to the country. Food and medicine are scarce, and Venezuelans are leaving their country in greater numbers than ever before. In 2014, journalist Rafael Osío Cabrices wrote, "This year we have in Venezuela, among our long list of wants, no shampoo, no elevator parts, no cancer medicines." Cabrices and his family emigrated to Montreal, Canada. He wrote, "As a resident of Canada, I feel like Princess Leia watching her home planet Alderaan explode from a window of the Death Star. I wish I could send some Millenium Falcon to rescue all my people."

In Colombia, even more people need rescuing. Civil war raged there for more than 50 years, finally coming to an end in 2016. During the war, almost eight million people fled. More people in Colombia have been displaced from their homes than in any other country. Many **refugees**, people who leave home to escape violence, settled in neighboring South

American countries. But others moved abroad. Colombian immigrants and refugees are the largest group of South Americans living in the United States. Their stories are harrowing. Ramiro Echeverri left after his father, a lawmaker, was kidnapped and killed in 2007. "We buried him and the next day we left the country," he said. They went to Ecuador and then to Atlanta, Georgia, where Echeverri now works as a medical researcher. For many South Americans, immigration offers an escape from difficult, desperate, or even terrifying circumstances. But not everyone who leaves the region is fleeing disaster. In the past few decades, South Americans have also been relocating abroad for higher education or to pursue careers in high-paying fields such as science, engineering, and medicine.

Economic difficulties in Venezuela in recent years have led to many protests like this one.

Maria Antoñiata Zegarra, who goes by Toñi, came to the United States from Peru in 2001 to complete her master's degree. She wound up staying in Massachusetts to work and raise a family. "I always wanted to have a life somewhere else," she says. "I always liked traveling and having new experiences."

Text-Dependent Questions:

1. Why is Japan a popular destination for people emigrating from Brazil?

2. What led to a boom in the Venezuela economy in the 20th century?

3. Which South American countries went through an economic crisis in the 1980s?

Research Project:

Choose a South American country. Look up the history of immigration to that country as well as emigration from there. What brought people to the country during the late 1800s and early 20th century? Where did they come from? Later in the 20th century, what events prompted people to leave?

STARTLING SPICES

Each Latin American country has its own unique food traditions. Even within a country, food varies from one region to the next. For example, people on the coast of Peru eat a lot of seafood, while those who live in the Andes Mountains eat more corn, potatoes, and meat. However, there are a few similarities that unite almost all Latin American food. One of the most important is flavor. Latin American cooks strive for depth and contrast in the flavors they use. And Latin American eaters try to taste all the different flavors at once. Maricel E. Presilla, author of a book on Latin American cooking, writes that people from this region tend to mix beans, meat, vegetables, sauces and more together in each bite. "They want lots of different tastes going on at once, so they can sense different layers of flavor above and beneath and beside each other."

In most Latin American cooking, the recipe begins with a technique that dates back to the Middle Ages in Spain, called a sofrito. It's a sautéed mix of flavorful ingredients, typically including onion and garlic. The rest of the meal builds on this foundation. Many recipes also use a complex blend of spices. In Brazil, the mix often contains garlic, vinegar or wine, cilantro, salt, black pepper, and a dash of very spicy pepper. In Peru, common spices include hot aji (AH-hee) peppers, cumin, oregano, and local herbs that aren't common elsewhere.

In Argentina, people often eat their meat with a spicy sauce called chimichurri which contains garlic, vinegar, dried hot peppers, and fresh herbs such as parsley. The zing in many Latin American dishes comes from peppers, a vegetable native to the Americas. "We love our many peppers, from the sweetest to the hottest," writes Presilla.

Settling In

Victor Alarcón came to America to join a sister-in-law who already lived there. Later, his wife and their sons joined him. His wife's mother eventually immigrated, too. Families often arrive in a new country this way, with one or two people helping to pave the way for others. The family doesn't always know when or

Words to Understand

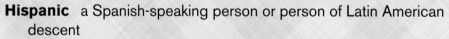

discrimination   unfair treatment of a group of people

Hispanic   a Spanish-speaking person or person of Latin American descent

illegal immigration   entering and staying in a country without permission

deportation   the forced removal of a person from a country

poverty   being very poor

racism   prejudice or hatred directed against a person solely because of his or her race or ethnicity

stereotype   a commonly held belief about a group of people that is not based on reason

This is a spicy meat stew from Brazil called a feijoada.

how they will be reunited, which is difficult and painful for all involved. Adjusting to life in a new country causes stress as well. Immigrants often don't speak the language and are unfamiliar with local customs and rules. Those who leave Latin America to escape **poverty** or violence typically don't have much money. They have to start from the bottom and work their way up. They may struggle to afford housing, transportation, and medical care.

This was the case for the Alarcón family. At first, they shared a small apartment with another family. Even after they got their own apartment, they still lived in an area where crime was a constant problem. One day,

The United States is debating the status of people covered by a US government program called Deferred Action for Childhood Arrivals (DACA).

gang members shot Victor Alarcón after he refused to let them push him around; he recovered, but later, the same gang came back and robbed the apartment. "I don't care if we don't have the money… we have to move," his wife said. The Alarcóns did move. Slowly and steadily, they accumulated enough savings, connections, and skills to succeed in America. Many South American immigrants have become successful citizens of other countries. But they all faced obstacles along the way.

Family Reunited

Like Alarcón, many Latin American immigrants follow family members to a new country. US law makes it much easier for people to immigrate if they already have family living in the country. This practice goes back

DACA

Daniela Vargas' parents brought her with them from Argentina in 2001, when she was seven years old. She went to school, made friends, and learned to speak English. Yet she risked deportation. So she took advantage of a US government program called Deferred Action for Childhood Arrivals (DACA). The program allowed people brought to the United States as children to avoid **deportation** and receive permission to work. In 2017, the US government chose to not renew the DACA program, though discussions and court cases are ongoing about what will happen to people who are part of it. After Vargas spoke out in defense of DACA, immigration agents kept her in jail for ten days. After her release, she said, "I wanted this country, or the president, to know that we are an asset to this country. We're not just here to steal jobs. We're here doing nice things. We're working. We're contributing. We're doing the best we can."

to the Immigration and Nationality Act, which President Lyndon Johnson signed into law in 1965. At the signing ceremony, he said, "This bill says simply that from this day forth, those wishing to immigrate to America shall be admitted on the basis of their skills and their close relationship to those already here." Previously, the United States had limited the number of people allowed to immigrate from specific countries. Nations in Europe were allowed much higher numbers of immigrants, a practice that discriminated against people on the basis of their race and ethnicity.

The new law was supposed to be much fairer to people of all backgrounds. Lawmakers also believed that making it easy for family members to immigrate would keep the dominant ethnic groups in the country the same. But that's not what happened. In the late 20th century, fewer Europeans wanted to immigrate. But many more Asians and Latin Americans were looking for a new start. After one person successfully immigrated, an entire extended family network could follow. Author Tom Gjelten notes in his book *Nation of Nations* that seven out of eight immigrants to the United States in 1960 were European. But by 2010, just one out of ten were from Europe. In 2013, most immigrants to the United States came from Mexico, Central America, India, China, and elsewhere in Asia. According to the Migration Policy Institute, 24 percent of the US population will be Hispanic by 2065.

Latino Culture

In the United States, South Americans may find themselves grouped in with the larger community of **Hispanics**. The terms Hispanic and Latino (or Latina for women) all refer to people with Latin American backgrounds. This includes immigrants from Mexico, Central America, Cuba, Puerto

Rico, and South America, as well as people from these family backgrounds who were born and raised in the United States. Many Latino people speak Spanish, follow the Catholic religion, and enjoy Latin American foods such as rice and beans or dishes flavored with hot peppers. However, an individual Latino person may not speak Spanish or belong to any religion. And that person may detest spicy food. Instead of calling herself Latina, a person may prefer to identify as Venezuelan. Or she may simply want to be called American.

Latinos are diverse people who come from many different cultural backgrounds. But certain similarities connect them. Janet Murguia, president of a Latino advocacy organization, says, "Culturally, we're bound by language, a common affection for Spanish—even though we learn English. Strong faith, strong family, strong sense of community— these are values we hold in common." But not everyone defines Latino culture in the same way. Sergio Bendixen, an expert in Hispanic politics

Future of Latino immigration

and media, says that country backgrounds, the Spanish language, and the Catholic religion aren't the most important factors. Rather, he says, Latino culture "gives tremendous weight to human relationships and the celebration of life; you are free to show your emotion, more than suppress your emotion."

Latinos also share a common burden. In America, **discrimination** and **racism** directed against Latino people remain a huge problem. According to a 2016 Pew Research Center survey, about half of Hispanic Americans say they have been treated unfairly due to their race or ethnicity. The

South American immigrants have found careers in many jobs, including entertainment and video journalism.

problem is especially bleak among young, nonwhite Hispanic Americans. They may end up excluded from jobs, treated poorly in public, or otherwise marginalized. Unfortunately, many Americans unfairly associate Latinos with crime, drugs, poverty, and **illegal immigration**. Immigrants from South America may fall victim to hateful treatment due to these **stereotypes**. Carlos Lozada remembers an elementary school classmate telling him, "Shut up, you stupid Mexican!" to which he responded, "Stupid *Peruvian*." But the fact that he was from Peru might not matter to someone who was biased against Latinos.

Family Separated

Many South American immigrants are legal residents of the United States. But others are not. Sometimes, illegal immigrants sneak across the border to get in. But more often, these immigrants enter the country legally on student, tourist, or temporary work visas, but end up staying longer than they were supposed to. There are many reasons why a person may stay on illegally. Rebeca, a television reporter from Venezuela, got into the United States on a tourist visa. She found work as a nanny and as a clothing designer. She feared returning to Venezuela because she had received death threats after participating in political protests there. But it will take years before immigration officials will consider whether to grant her permission to stay.

Jesús Jave-Castillo trekked from Peru all the way across the Mexican border in 2000. From there, he went on to Miami, Florida. His father needed medical care that the family couldn't afford, and he hoped to earn money in the United States to send home. He managed to find work in the landscaping business. Three years later, his brother Jenry joined him. After another five years, Jenry had started his own landscaping business and purchased a nice home. However, the brothers never obtained permission to live in the United States. They were breaking the law by staying and working in Miami. If the government caught them, they could be deported, meaning they'd have to move back to Peru. Jenry decided to solve this problem in an unusual way. He got married to an American citizen. His family only found out about the arrangement after Jenry died suddenly of a heart attack at 38. Jesús believes that the marriage wasn't real—his brother did it to try to become a legal immigrant.

Colombian actress Diane Guerrero

Marrying someone to obtain legal status is a risky arrangement. But illegal immigrants face a slew of problems, and are often willing to take drastic measures to become legal. Many jobs aren't open to them. They constantly fear deportation, and may avoid seeking help from the police or at a hospital.

Deportation can break families apart, as actress Diane Guerrero, one of the stars of the TV series *Orange Is the New Black*, knows all too well. "I am the citizen daughter of immigrant parents who were deported when I was 14. My older brother was also deported," she said. Guerrero's parents came from

Colombia to escape poverty before she was born. For years, her parents tried to become legal immigrants. Then one day, "I came home from school to an empty house. Lights were on and dinner had been started, but my family wasn't there. Neighbors broke the news that my parents had been taken away by immigration officers, and just like that, my stable family life was over." Her brother had to leave behind his wife and young daughter. Guerrero lived with friends throughout high school and college, and managed to find success as an actress, but others in her situation haven't been so lucky. When families are broken apart, the stress causes some to make bad choices. Guerrero's brother's daughter later wound up in jail.

Adjusting to life in a new country is hard enough for a person who has permission to stay and work. Illegal status complicates life for some South American immigrants and their families.

Text-Dependent Questions:

1. Under the 1965 Immigration and Nationality Act, what makes someone a candidate for immigration to the United States?

2. How might discrimination or racism affect a Latino person's life?

3. How do most illegal immigrants get into the United States?

Research Project:

Many South Americans identify with Latino culture. Choose one of the following: Latino music, art, or literature. Research its history and find a prominent South American who contributed to the field.

THE STAPLES: RICE, CORN, BEANS, AND POTATOES

What ends up piled high on a person's dinner plate almost every night in South America? The answer depends on where that person is. Corn, potatoes, rice, beans, and yucca, a type of root, are all staple foods in different parts of the continent. In certain regions of South America, people regularly add sweet potatoes, yams, squash, quinoa, or plantains to their plates.

Corn was originally cultivated in the Americas over 5,000 years ago. In South America, people use corn to make arepas, a type of cornbread, and chicha, a corn-based drink. Peruvians snack on corn kernels that are toasted like popcorn. Potatoes also originally come from South America. In the Andes Mountains, farmers grow these tubers in an amazing variety of colors and shapes. In the winter in the Andes Mountains, it's traditional to leave potatoes outside until they freeze. Then the potatoes are boiled and eaten with cheese.

In Brazil, the staple food of choice is yucca, also called cassava. This root is ground into flour and used in a variety of dishes, including farofa, *a fluffy Brazilian side dish that's somewhat similar to stuffing.*

Rice isn't a native food in South America. The Spanish and Portuguese brought it with them. But rice has become an essential part of the cuisine in many South American countries. Toñi Zegarra says her family has rice and potatoes with almost every meal. She says, "My husband is crazy about rice. If he doesn't see rice on the side of the dish, it's not complete." Potatoes are essential, too. Her kids love one meal she makes that's a variation on spaghetti. She makes pasta with meat sauce, and puts french fries on top.

In many parts of Latin America as well as in Africa and the Caribbean, people eat rice and beans together. Black beans are most popular in Brazil and Venezuela, while red beans are a staple in Colombia.

3

Connecting

Orlando Tobón was born in a small town in Colombia. He came to New York City in 1968 because he was fascinated by the United States. He wound up getting a work visa and a job at a factory. At night, he studied accounting. As he moved up in the world, he began bringing family members over. He wasn't the only one doing this. A small community of Colombian Americans gradually grew bigger. Today, around 20,000 Colombians live in one neighborhood in Queens county in New York City. The area is known as Little Colombia. And Tobón is their unofficial mayor. He makes a living working as an accountant who prepares tax returns. But he also goes out of his way to help fellow Colombian Americans navigate

Words to Understand

assimilate   to adapt or adjust to a new place, idea, or culture

citizenship   the status of being an official member of a country

immersed   deeply involved in something

Quechua   a family of Native American languages spoken in the Andes Mountains of South America

vibrant   full of energy, color, and life

The Colombian flag flutters above a historic fort in Cartagena.

tricky situations. In one week, he helped a woman translate a **citizenship** application. He assisted another woman who had recently gotten out of prison. He got a wheelchair from someone who didn't need it anymore in order and gave it to someone else who did. "People from Colombia get off the plane, and they have one phone number, and it's Orlando's," says Arturo-Ignacio Sánchez, an expert in immigrant communities at Cornell University. "There are Orlandos in almost every immigrant community."

Welcome to the Neighborhood

Communities of South American immigrants can be found all around the globe. These communities offer new immigrants a place to live that feels more like the home they left behind. In an immigrant community, people can speak their native language, shop at grocery stores with foods from their home country, and get assistance from people like Tobón who have already been living in the area for a long time. The town of Oizumi, just north of Tokyo, Japan, is known as Brazilian Town. Around one-tenth of the town's population is from Brazil. In the restaurant and grocery store Casa Blanca, everyone speaks Portuguese. Guests pile their plates with black bean stew, steak with caramelized onions, and potato salad from a buffet. They guzzle down cans of Guarana Antarctica, a Brazilian soft drink with twice as much caffeine as coffee.

The city of Paterson, New Jersey, is home to an estimated 10,000 to 30,000 Peruvians. They have set up restaurants, bakeries, hair salons, travel agencies, automotive shops, and more. Some call their area of town Little Lima, after the capital of Peru. Every year since 1986, the community has held a giant Peruvian Day Parade. And in 2016, the city officially named one part of the city Peru Square. "This city is better because Peruvians decided to call it home," said councilman Andre Sayegh at the naming celebration.

Several thousand people from Ecuador have settled in the small town of Milford, Massachusetts. Many of these immigrants speak **Quechua**, a native language of the Andes Mountains, rather than Spanish. In the Andes, guinea pigs are raised not as pets but for food. At an Ecuadorian restaurant in Milford, cook Jessica Brito prepares guinea pigs with a spice paste of onion, garlic, cumin, and salt. A Catholic church serves as a focal point for the Ecuadorian community in Milford. Some of the priests help run an organization called Health, Education, and Advocacy for Latinos (HEAL). It offers English classes, health classes, and counseling for immigrants.

A parade like this one honoring Peru's history and customs is held annually in Paterson, New Jersey, home to a large Peruvian community.

The Capital of Latin America

One of the most **vibrant** and diverse Latino communities in the world can be found in Miami, Florida. The coastal city, sometimes called the capital of Latin America, is just 100 miles from the island nation of Cuba. After a revolution there in the 1950s, many Cubans fled on boats bound for Florida. Over the decades, people from other Latin American nations followed. The city is now 70 percent Hispanic. Almost 51 percent of the residents were born in a foreign country, according to Guillermo Grenier, a sociologist at Florida International University. Miami is one of the top destinations for wealthy, educated South Americans. "If you are a business owner in Latin America, you can come to Miami, you have an

This area of Miami, Florida, is the center of a large Cuban community.

audience, a market, you can make five calls, in Spanish, and set up the infrastructure for your business," says Grenier.

Luis Arias is a doctor originally from Venezuela who now lives in Miami. He says, "I like that I'm surrounded by other Latin people. You have access to all the things you enjoy in your country while being in the United States." Juan Pablo Restrepo agrees with these sentiments. A Miami resident originally from Colombia, Restrepo lives with his family in a nice neighborhood near the beach and works for a media company. "Miami is very attractive for Latin Americans," he says. "They get to be in the United States, with all its advantages, but keeping familiar cultural roots." He continues, "If you go to other places in the country, you feel the cultural and racial tensions to a much larger degree."

A New Language

In most parts of Miami, residents can get through the day without speaking a word of English. Spanish is rapidly becoming the dominant language in the city. But this isn't the case for many other cities where South American immigrants settle. Young children of immigrants typically master a new language quickly. But adults often struggle. They may depend on their children to translate, or may separate themselves from the host culture in an immigrant community. In America, programs such as HEAL offer a way for immigrants to learn English. Ecuadorian Narcisa Mayancela attends HEAL's classes. She says, "Wednesdays and Thursdays I go to English class. I bring my kids. Thank God they take care of my children, so I can study."

In the 1980s through the early 2000s, there were so many children growing up in the United States speaking both Spanish and English that they began

A Taste of South America in Miami

Restaurants and grocery stores that offer authentic South American foods abound in Miami. Nick Garcia, a photographer originally from Colombia who now lives in Miami, enjoys going out for a taste of home. One of his favorites is fish served with coconut rice and fried plantains. His favorite restaurants "are very relaxed and laid-back," he says. "You don't need to dress up or make reservations; it feels almost like visiting family." Daniela Ramirez, a fashion blogger originally from Venezuela, enjoys arepas, a traditional flatbread made mainly from cornmeal. They are often served stuffed with fillings, such as shredded beef, rice, and cheese. She says, "Every dish on a Venezuelan menu is completely different from the next, but all have special flavors that remind me of home." A Peruvian restaurant in Miami serves more than 15 styles of ceviche, a seafood dish that features raw fish or shellfish marinated in lime or lemon juice.

mixing the two languages together, creating a hybrid informally known as Spanglish. Fifteen-year-old Ilyn explained how it works to the BBC, "Por ejemplo, I'm talking with my friends and sometimes Spanish gets mixed in with the English and you're like, hey, como estas, I saw you the other day..." Spanglish also includes hybrid words, such as *hanguer*, which is "hang out" with a Spanish verb ending. However, Spanglish seems to be fading from popularity now as fewer new immigrants are arriving from Latin America. English is gradually becoming the language of choice for

Latinos in the United States. In 2015, the Pew Hispanic Center found that 71 percent of Hispanics in the United States didn't believe that speaking Spanish was a necessary part of a Latino identity.

A Short Blanket

Language isn't the only difficulty for immigrants. Living far from family and familiar traditions causes stress and sadness. New social and cultural customs may seem strange. But over time, most people manage to adapt. When Toñi Zegarra arrived, she found American meal times unusual. "In Peru, lunch time is not earlier than 1:30 or 2; dinner is around 8 or 9." Also, even though her kids were born in the United States, she never taught them to eat sandwiches for lunch. "When they go to school, they don't enjoy having a cold sandwich," she says. They want her to make Peruvian dishes. So she packs pasta or another dish into a thermos to keep it warm.

Hispanic impact on the United States

Mariana, who prefers to use only her first name, came to the United States from Argentina in 2007 to earn her master's degree and later a PhD. She never intended to stay, but then she met and married her husband, who is American. "Living in another country is like having a short blanket," she says, using a common Argentine saying. She explains, "If you cover your feet, your torso is not covered. If you cover your torso, your feet are exposed. I can never feel like I'm really home." One difference she noticed was in the way people greet each other. In Argentina, friends would hug

Sipping Mate Together

Instead of coffee, many people from Argentina, Uruguay, Paraguay, Southern Brazil, and Bolivia drink a form of tea called mate (MAH-tay). To make mate, a person puts dried leaves of the yerba mate plant into a gourd or small mug. Then, he or she pours a small amount of near-boiling water over the leaves and sips from a straw until the liquid is gone. Then, more water is added. If friends are together, the cup gets passed around. "Mate is more than just a drink," says Mariana. "You share the straw." Drinking mate together indicates hospitality and friendship. Mate also provides an energy boost similar to coffee. Mariana drinks mate almost every day. "When I'm more homesick or stressed out, I drink more mate," she says.

and kiss, and she missed those friendly greetings, especially during her first six months in the United States. Still, she knew it was important to **assimilate** as best she could, and spent most of her time with Americans. The more time an immigrant spends around local people and **immersed** in the new culture, the faster he or she will learn to speak the new language, follow new customs, and feel at home in a new land.

Text-Dependent Questions:

1. What are three reasons why a new immigrant might settle in a community of other immigrants from the same country?

2. What percentage of the population of Miami, Florida, is Hispanic?

3. What is Spanglish?

Research Project:

Find a restaurant in Miami that serves South American food and has an online menu. (Hint: Search for "Peruvian restaurant in Miami" or "Brazilian restaurant in Miami.") Choose an item on the menu and look up the history of the dish. What cultures influenced the dish? Look especially for Spanish, Portuguese, Native American, and African influences.

AUTHENTIC LATIN AMERICAN FAVORITES

To those unfamiliar with Latin American cultures, Latin food probably means tacos, burritos, and nachos. These popular foods are served in restaurants across the United States. Yet all three were invented in the United States. Some examples of true Latin American foods include empanadas, tamales, and grilled meat.

Empanadas are like little pies stuffed with meat, typically beef, or other fillings. The Spanish brought empanadas with them to the New World, adapting the recipe as needed to include local ingredients. For example, the dough may be made from corn, yucca, or plantain flour. In the Caribbean, empanadas tend to be fried, but in Chile and Argentina, cooks bake them in the oven. Empanadas are most often eaten as appetizers or snacks. Bolivians enjoy a type of empanada that is both sweet and spicy.

Cooking myths and superstitions have a long history in Latin America. Here are some common ones.
- *Never stir or taste anything with a knife—this invites trouble.*
- *Sprinkle salt into the cooking pot in the shape of a cross.*
- *Tamales will not cook right if a twin looks at them.*
- *Don't allow anyone who might have the "evil eye" into the kitchen.*

Tamales consist of dough and other fillings cooked inside a corn husk or banana leaves. The dish originated with the native peoples of North and South America. Different countries and regions make different kinds of tamales. Today, since tamales are time-consuming to make, people mainly have them for birthdays, weddings, or holidays. Venezuelans make large tamales for Christmas. In Peru, Ecuador, Chile, and parts of Argentina, people make a version of tamale called a humita. It can be sweet and filled with raisins and sugar or savory and stuffed with cheese or chicken.

Grilling, also known as barbecue, is a huge part of South American cooking, especially in Argentina, Colombia, Venezuela, and Brazil. Most cooks use a flat outdoor grill called a parilla. It's usually built into a chimney-like structure alongside the house. "In Argentina, every house comes with that; it's a must," says Mariana. In the countryside, people may dig a pit and roast large pieces of beef, pork, lamb or goat on a skewer instead. It's common to eat all parts of the animal. Maricel E. Presilla describes a mixed grill that a Uruguayan friend prepared for her. The meats included "tripe, udder, sweetbreads, a whole kidney, beef ribs cut into strips, skirt steak, Argentine pork, and even bull's testicles."

4

Reaching Back

Mariana will soon visit Argentina with her young daughter. It will be her daughter's first trip to the country. "I can't wait," Mariana says. They will celebrate Christmas with her family there. Since Argentina is in the Southern Hemisphere, Christmas falls in the middle of the summer. "It's like the Fourth of July," says Mariana. People eat dinner outside on long tables. Some have pool parties. They set off fireworks at midnight. But they also put up Christmas trees and exchange gifts, just like in America. Mariana is looking forward to introducing her daughter to the sights, sounds, smells, and tastes of her hometown. But she realizes that her daughter is American. She will grow up knowing American culture as her own. But like many immigrant parents, Mariana hopes her daughter will appreciate and enjoy her Argentine heritage.

Words to Understand

integrate   to gradually become an equal and participating part of a group

limbo   a period of uncertainty

remittance   money sent as a gift to friends and family back home

Inspired by scenes like this church in Argentina lit up for Christmas, South Americans living elsewhere carry on long-held traditions.

Keeping in Touch

Even after immigrants make the move to a new country, they remain forever linked to the home they left behind. Today, it's easier than ever for immigrants to stay connected with friends, family, and cultural traditions back home. Regular communication through social media, video calls, texts, and more helps ease the pain of separation from loved ones. Journalist Martin Barrow emigrated from South America to Great Britain before mobile phones and the internet. "My only contact with family and friends was by post, which took several weeks," he writes. "The telephone

At a festival in London, Brazilians living in that British capital city celebrate the culture of their home far away.

was prohibitively expensive and unreliable. There was no online news to keep up-to-date with events at home, so I soon lost touch. Without social media, it was fiendishly difficult to find other people from South America." Since he couldn't maintain a connection, Barrow had no choice but to learn English and **integrate** into British culture.

Today, everything is different. Barrow has watched a woman from Colombia FaceTime her family as she starts her cleaning shift. He's also noticed a Peruvian business owner watching Latin American soap operas on her laptop while keeping an eye on her shop. Barrow says, "The immigrant of

 ## Sending Money Home

Many South American immigrants leave to escape financial difficulty. They plan to work to earn money and better their family's situation. Often, they regularly send money or goods, called **remittances**, to family back home. Lucia Jimenez lives in Spain but sends money to her children in her home country of Paraguay. In 2015, South American citizens received almost $15 billion in remittances, according to the Migration Policy Institute. This money is mainly spent on food, housing, and clothing. In Spain, Ecuadorians make up the largest group of South American immigrants. Shops in Madrid and Barcelona allow people to purchase appliances for delivery to Ecuador. And one company plans to open ATMs that will allow people in Spain to pay for groceries, medicine, or cell phones in Ecuador.

today, however difficult his circumstances may be, is rarely disconnected from his home, his culture or his language for long." Even immigrants who don't live around others from their same background always have a virtual community to turn to. This may make some immigrants less likely to fully integrate into the new culture and community. But it also makes it easier to maintain a connection to more than one nation.

Bridging Cultures

After a long enough time in a new country, though, its culture may start to feel more familiar than the one that was left behind. Edmundo Arroyo-Fuentes brought his family to Canada from Chile in 1979 to escape the dictatorship there. Once the political situation in the country improved, Arroyo-Fuentes started visiting Chile again. But things were different. "We realized we were strangers in our own country, both with our families and among our friends," he says.

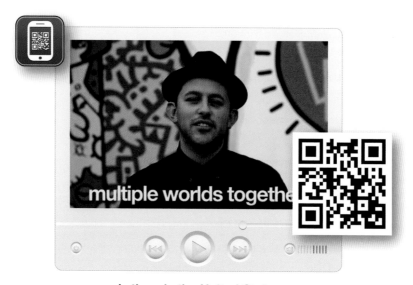

Latinos in the United States

This feeling of not fully belonging in the country of origin is usually strongest for immigrants' children. They grow up in the new country, bridging two cultures. Often, they speak two languages and enjoy foods, holidays, and other traditions from both cultures. Toñi Zegarra's children are old enough to understand this fact. Zegarra and her husband, who is also Peruvian, told them, "You are Americans, but you are also Peruvians. You are very lucky you can have both sides. That brings you another language and gives you a different perspective. You know the world is not

Returning to Japan?

Not all immigrants stay in their new home. Many eventually decide to return. Usually, they do so in their own lifetimes. But sometimes the family returns after several generations.

Recently, many Japanese Brazilians, born and raised in Brazil, have made the choice to move their families to Japan. These immigrants often look Japanese, but they don't speak the language or behave according to Japanese social customs. This can cause confusion about a person's identity. Bruno, a Japanese Brazilian boy, arrived in Japan at age five. By the time he was in high school, he spoke fluent Japanese. "In the future, I want to live here in Japan," he said. "But if I have money and vacation time, I'd like to return to Brazil once, to travel and see my grandma and aunt. I haven't seen them in about ten years." When it comes to his identity, though, he says, "I identify as Brazilian."

only the way it is in the United States. There are other cultures." Zegarra hopes that when her children grow up, they learn to embrace both Peruvian and American traditions. "I hope they make their own culture," she says.

Annie, a lifestyle blogger who prefers not to use her last name, knows how growing up in two cultures can expand a person's horizons. She came to America from Colombia when she was 13. She says, "While I still enjoy some Latin media and we've always spoken Spanish at home (with a few phrases in English in between), the truth is that I love American TV, movies, and music. In fact, in a given week, I may listen to just one Latin song but hundreds of American ones." If she had only grown up in one of her two cultures, she might never have known about the other one's music and movies.

Who Am I?

Being a part of two worlds is a unique and special experience for immigrants and their children. But it can also be confusing. Cristian Delgado came to Sweden from Chile when he was eight years old. "I speak better Swedish than Spanish," he says. "Yet when someone speaks to me here, the first thing they say is, 'Where are you from?'" He knows that his children will face similar questions because of their names and the way they look. "There's going to be an identity conflict there," he says. His children may not feel as if they fully belong in either Sweden or Chile.

Victor Alarcón's son Álvaro can identify with this problem. By the time he graduated from high school, he preferred to speak English. He had returned to Bolivia only once, when he was nine years old, and he never wanted to go back. In the United States, he'd gotten used to celebrating holidays like Thanksgiving and Christmas the American way. His family had turkey, mashed potatoes, and cranberries instead of Bolivian food. Yet people always asked where he was from, which to him meant they didn't believe he was really American. "I feel like I'm in **limbo**," he says. "I can't say I'm Bolivian, because I don't know anything about the place, but I can't say I'm American, because I wasn't born here. So when people ask me where I'm from, I can't give a straight answer."

Álvaro's family settled in Fairfax County, Virginia, just west of Washington, DC. This area has become a haven for immigrants from all corners of the globe. In the year 2000, one in four residents of the county was an immigrant, and students in the schools spoke over 100 different languages. Álvaro found that he identified most closely not with other Hispanic teens in the area, but with other immigrants who had arrived at a similar age as him. His two best friends were Fasih Khan, originally from Pakistan, and Ho-Kwon, originally from South Korea. Ho-Kwon

A woman models Bolivian traditional clothing at a cultural festival in Virginia.

says, "We used to get a kick out of thinking how strange we probably seemed to people. I mean, people would look at us and see a 'Chinese' guy, a 'Spanish' guy, and a 'Middle Eastern' guy coming into a store together. How often did people see that? We joked about it all the time." They also shared food. Fasih was visiting the Alarcóns' house one day and found a familiar spice mix in the cupboard—one used in Pakistani and Indian cooking. Álvaro had tasted it at Fasih's house, and liked it so much that he and his parents started cooking with it.

Álvaro's story shows that a person's name or nationality doesn't reveal as much about that person as others might think. Álvaro's

Whether barbecuing South American dishes or holding an all-American hot dog cookout, immigrant families are part of the fabric of America.

personality, family, friends, and upbringing matter more than broad labels like "Bolivian" or "Latino." Immigrants combine experiences and personal connections from two or more cultures, allowing them a broader view of the world and each person's place in it.

Text-Dependent Questions:

1. What is Christmas like in Argentina?

2. How do immigrants today keep in touch with family back home?

3. Why might an immigrant's children become confused about their cultural identity?

Research Project:

Look into your own family history. What cultures are part of your family's past? How do these cultures affect your family's lifestyle and celebrations? How would you describe your cultural identity? What makes you feel proud of the culture or cultures that you identify with?

DESSERT

Chocolate and vanilla, two of the most essential dessert ingredients, both originated in South America. But they were not originally used in in sweet foods. Rather, they made strong-tasting drinks out of them. Then the Spanish started running sugar cane plantations throughout the region. Latin Americans took to sugar in a big way. "Latin American desserts are very, very sweet," writes Maricel E. Presilla.

The Spanish and Portuguese introduced a tradition of cooking sugar with milk, eggs, or both to make thick puddings or sauces. One of the most popular in Latin America is dulce de leche, a kind of caramel made from milk and sugar. In Argentina, Peru, and Uruguay, people love powdery cookies called alfajores that are filled with dulce de leche. South Americans also spread dulce de leche on all sorts of breads, pastries, and cakes.

In addition to sugary caramels and pastries, Latin Americans adore fresh fruit or fruit-based desserts. The tropical rain forests supply a huge range of fruit. "Mango, papaya, pineapple, bananas, they all grow here," says Toñi Zegarra. South Americans also enjoy a huge variety of tropical fruits not common in the rest of the world, from naranjilla, *which resembles a small orange, to* cherimoya, *a green fruit with a creamy inside (below).*

Alfajores de Maizena
Traditional cookies from Argentina

Ingredients:

7/8 cups butter (almost 2 sticks), softened
5/8 cup sugar
1 tsp lemon or orange zest
1 tsp vanilla extract
3 egg yolks
1 1/4 cups cornstarch
1 tsp baking soda
1 1/2 tsp baking powder
pinch of salt
7/8 cups flour
2 cups dulce de leche, for filling cookies
powdered sugar, coconut flakes, or melted chocolate (optional)

Directions:

1. Preheat oven to 350°F.
2. Mix butter with sugar by hand or in a mixer until light and fluffy.
3. Add zest, vanilla extract, and then egg yolks, one at a time, mixing well after each addition.
4. In a large bowl, mix the cornstarch, baking soda, baking powder, and salt. Sift in the flour and mix well.
5. Add the dry ingredients to the egg mixture. Mix very briefly. Do not work the dough!
6. Wrap the dough in foil and refrigerate for 15–20 minutes.
7. Roll the dough flat until it is about 1/4 inch thick.
8. Use round cookie cutters or a round jar lid to punch out cookies about 2–3 inches across. Reroll dough as needed.
9. Place the cookies at least 1/2 inch apart on ungreased baking sheets.
10. Bake for about 15 minutes, until firm on the bottom (The cookies should still look pale). Transfer cookies to a rack and allow to cool.
11. Flip half of the cookies over and spread dulce de leche on each. Place another cookie on top to make a sandwich.
12. Spread dulce de leche along the sides of each sandwich and roll in powdered sugar, coconut, or melted chocolate.

Find Out More

Books

Barnett, Tracy L. *Immigration from South America.* Broomall, PA: Mason Crest Publishers Inc., 2004.

DePietro, Frank. *South American Immigrants.* Broomall, PA: Mason Crest Publishers Inc., 2013.

Gjelten, Tom. *A Nation of Nations: A Great American Immigration Story.* New York: Simon and Schuster, 2015.

McIntosh, Kenneth and Marsha. *South America's Immigrants to the United States: The Flight from Turmoil.* Broomall, PA: Mason Crest Publishers Inc, 2006.

Presilla, Maricel E. *Gran Cocina Latina: The Food of Latin America.* New York: W. W. Norton & Company, 2012.

Websites

https://www.migrationpolicy.org/
Learn about Latin American immigration to the United States, Europe, and elsewhere on this informative website.

https://www.telesurtv.net/english/analysis/Chronicling-the-Diaspora-South-America-20171007-0015.html
Discover the history of South American immigration.

https://www.thespruce.com/introduction-to-south-american-food-3029236
Find recipes for authentic South American food on this website.

Series Glossary of Key Terms

acclimate to get used to something

assimilate become part of a different society, country, or group

bigotry treating the members of a racial or ethnic group with hatred and intolerance

culinary having to do with the preparing of food

diaspora a group of people who live outside the area in which they had lived for a long time or in which their ancestors lived

emigrate leave one's home country to live in another country

exodus a mass departure of people from one place to another

first-generation American someone born in the United States whose parents were foreign born

immigrants those who enter another country intending to stay permanently

naturalize to gain citizenship, with all its rights and privileges

oppression a system of forcing people to follow rules or a system that restricts freedoms

presentation in this series, the style in which food is plated and served

Index

Photo Credits

Dreamstime.com: Peter Hermes Furian 7; Samystclair 8; Martin Schneiter 9; Jesse Kraft 11, 17; Americanspirit 12; Sergey Mayorov 13; Alf Ribiero 14; Carlos de Bon 16; Oliver Förstner 18; Edgloris Marys 20; Elena Veselova 23; Luz Ribiero 25; Andrei Gabriel Stanescu 26; Kadettman 30; Julie Feinstein 34; Rodrigo De Souza Mendes Junquiera 34, 35; Eq Roy 40; Lostafichuk 42; Natalia Yaumenenka 44; Adwo 46; Pablo Hidalgo 47; Shawn Goldberg 49; Desislava Vasielva 50; Sretanka Moraca 51; Teresa Kenney 55; Blend Images 56; Betochagas 58; Gavin Echterling 59T; Pavlo Baliukh 59B; Rimma Bondarenko 60T; Natushm 60B. FusionCraftiness.com: 22. Shutterstock: Jannis Tobias Wenner 37. Wikimedia CC: Larry D. Moore 32; Mori Phoenix 53.

Author Bio

Kathryn Hulick is a freelance writer and former Peace Corps volunteer. For two years, she lived in Kyrgyzstan, a small country that borders China and Russia. There, she experienced first-hand what it's like to try to get used to a new language, culture, and foods. She ate a lot of mutton and potatoes! When she returned to the United States, she started writing for children. Her books include: *Hydrogen* and *Gold* in the Chemistry of Everyday Elements series and *My Teenage Life in Russia*. She also contributes regularly to *Muse* magazine and the Science News for Students website. She enjoys hiking, painting, reading, and working in her garden. Learn more about her work at kathrynhulick.com.